The Turn Around

MARRIAGE, MINISTRY AND HEALTH

The Turn Around

MARRIAGE, MINISTRY AND HEALTH

Thomas and Carolyn Little

Lifestyle Soulutions
Fishers, Indiana
2016

Unless otherwise indicated, all Scripture quotations are taken from the King James Version of the Bible.

Cover by Be Bold Publishing Grand Rapids Michigan

Layout Design by Jagari Publishing Company, LLC, Orlando, Florida

THE TURN AROUND: MARRIAGE, MINISTRY AND HEALTH

ISBN: 978-0-692-82419-1

Printed in the United States of America

Dedication

Thank you, Lord!

We dedicate this restoration story to everyone that desires to make what seems impossible possible.

A special thanks to all who believed beyond all doubts!

Thank you to our parents; Thomas J. Little, Sr., Dorothy J. Little, Bessie Pryor and Richard H. Davis, Jr. (R.I.H.).

Thank you to our pastors, friends and relatives for sharing this journey with us.

This book would not be possible without our beautiful children Eric, Kristian, Robert, Jennifer, Charmaine, and Joseph; our eight amazing grandchildren, and our great grandson.

We love you all and may you continue in God's blessings and favor!

Thomas and Carolyn Little

Foreword

It's hard to imagine two better people who can bring practical wisdom to those who are considering or who have experienced divorce. Thomas and Carolyn Little were married, divorced, then pursued a path of restoration that led to their remarriage that has lasted over 17 years. Not only have I had the privilege of knowing them personally, I have been able to observe their family and witness their ministry. The Littles are full of wisdom and have a proven track record of consistency in applying God's principles of relationship success through the trials of conflict, addiction and major health complications. They know how to keep it real and yet keep it refreshing. I have no doubt that the principles contained in this book will inspire and give you practical help on how to build and restore a marriage.

Pastor Darryn Scheske, Founding &Senior Pastor
Heartlamd Church, Indiana Indianapolis

"God Turned It"
Inspired by Tye Tribett's He Turned It

Yes there were times in my life when I thought I would never make it.
I almost went down I was out for the count I was through.
But it was then when I thought it would end that I stood up again and
What hell had for evil God turned it around for my good.

The devil thought he had me,
Marriage destroyed, kicked out of Ministry and consequences of my
Choices led to what was at the time an incurable disease, Hep C.

Thought that my life was (over)
He thought by now I'd (give up)
He thought I had no (more)-ready to throw in the towel, going through the motions
only because I was alive, hopeless, helpless and almost heartless
But that's when someone (greater)
Stepped in my (situation)
My restoration has now begun...
GOD TURNED IT!

Sometimes I look back and I don't know how in the world I made it
All of those nights I would cried my heart so filled with pain
Not knowing if my husband was dead or alive, what would happen to my children,
facing the dishonor daily,
Worry consumed me my whole life revolved around fear and stress, my children and I
made vulnerable to a dangerous environment, becoming a single parent, having to live
off of one income
I was tired and weak I just could not compete anymore with drugs

The devil thought he (had me)-thought he had my mind, will and emotions
Thought that my life was (over)-thought that I could not recover

He thought by now I'd (give up)-
He thought I had no (more)
But that's when someone (greater)
Stepped in my (situation)
My new life now begun...

Because GOD TURNED IT!

He turned my mourning into dancing
He turned my sorrows into joy!

No more crying days
No more hurt and pain
No more guilt and shame
God turned it!
No more loneliness
No more fear and stress
No more sad events
GOD TURNED IT!

Table of Contents

INTRODUCTION

Carolyn:

Let's talk about the "d" word: divorce. While two people use it as a tool to break a contract, it can impact so many others, including family and friends. There are times when divorce is necessary, but not when it came to us. While at the time there seemed to be no other option but divorce, Thomas and I later realized if two people are willing to change, forgive, and truly move forward, they can overcome the obstacles that can tear families apart. For example, financial issues (especially when the wife is the "bread winner" or making more money than the husband), infidelity, verbal and physical abuse can be detrimental to marriages that result in divorce.

Financial issues adversely presented an obstacle in our marriage. Thomas attacked our bank account with a vengeance. He was on a binge and made several withdrawals in a short period of time. I noticed this and actually showed up at the ATM when he was about to hit it again! He stopped dead in his tracks!!! I could not understand why we continued to have overdraft fees, so I went inside the branch to speak with a manager. Here's the lunacy that accompanies the selfishness. Thomas, the bank manager and I reviewed film of the person withdrawing the money and it was Thomas. We sat in front of the bank officer and Thomas swore the picture of the man making withdrawals was not him. The bank officer looked at the picture, then at Thomas, they looked back at the picture and at Thomas again. Apparently in disbelief, they shook their head and left. This incident is one we will not forget. Thomas' selfish attitude caused our inability to communicate; communication was non-existent.

Thomas: This situation destroyed any commitment possibilities to be accessible and proved that my desire to be high overshadowed any love I really had for God, family or self. I had to confront my selfish heart to overcome those desires. I had to be "turned around" to become the true me: man of God, caring father, loving son and trusted husband.

Another marital obstacle that can tear families apart is infidelity. We believe marriage is between one man and one woman, but we have seen marriages and families destroyed because of infidelity. Infidelity, however, was not a problem in our marriage.

I saw firsthand of examples of adulterous relationships that broke the most prominent families down, so I was an advocate for faithfulness in marriage. Now my drug affair brought about a conflict. Drugs and women went together and I was deep into drugs; however my spiritual conflict stopped me from getting involved with the sex and drug culture successfully. I just could not enjoy being with anyone but Carolyn. Now I know our bodies cry out for pleasure and I am no different than any other man, but I'm just explaining my facts. I felt so guilty whenever I was involved with someone else, that for me, it was just easier to get high and deal with those consequences. Later, while living in Alabama and Michigan and during our five year separation as a sober man, I had opportunities to be involved with other women. There were times before and after the divorce was final where relationships were possible, but in my heart of hearts I was still married to Carolyn. Counselors and friends declared Carolyn was gone and encouraged me to move on with my life. They wanted to introduce me to good Godly women who might just be a good fit for a minister. Women who thought "God has sent their Boaz" were looking for a Godly man and me, being a preacher, I met the criterion for sure. Nevertheless, there was a battle between my soul (mind, intellect, will, imagination and emotions) and my spirit. My mind said, she's gone—go on with your life. My intellect said think before you act, and my will was all over the place. My imagination was saying things I won't even write down. My emotions wanted to be in a relationship. My soul was all over the place! But my spirit was direct, unwavering, uncompromising, and unsatisfied with anything but having my family back together.

There were opportunities to date, but I was unable to do so with good a conscience. I had a desire that fueled my faith. That's when a good friend who was the women's director at the ministry I was pastoring at said these prophetic words, "Pastor Tom, you want your family back, then act like it." Now hopefully this helps someone who is fighting for their family. This tactic was actually a killer blow to the enemy and his plans. I took this strategy and it propelled me into an ongoing onslaught of faithfulness to God, family and me! I acted as if I were still married to Carolyn! No women, no dates, no sex partners, nothing but God and family. My time went to ministry and spending time with my kids.

I take responsibility for being immature and selfish, but I also take credit for accepting the responsibility to change those things so that divorce was not the answer for us. To get straight to the point, my drug abuse was just an obstacle that led to many other issues. I had to realize that I liked being high. The realization allowed me to fight the issue. When I overcame the challenge and the love for drugs by the grace of God, I could make a decision to choose what I really loved - God, Carolyn, my family, and most importantly myself. I began to focus on living a life that I knew was not only better for me but profitable to others.

I must admit I can't take all the credit for the restoration of our marriage. All my efforts to prove I had changed failed. Carolyn had declared too many times that she would not even consider remarrying me unless God spoke to her and said "Tom is your husband AGAIN!!!" So I focused on maintaining and building my relationship with my kids, helping others with problems like mine, and simply loving my life. I allowed God to do His part, to touch her heart. I had always said

Carolyn is divorced, but I'm still married to her. So I acted like I was still married; I wasn't living with her or involved in her decisions, but I was there if I was ever needed. Today I'm just grateful to have been an example of a restoration story. God did the rest. Now the obstacles of infidelity, communication and financial instability have been overcome and are no longer an issue. To put it another way, they are a "non-factor"!!!

Divorce can be overcome. Families can be recovered by forgiveness, communication, and teamwork. These are the things that led to our restoration.

This is the result of finding out
When Divorce is Not the Answer,
but
Restoration Is A Process.

CHAPTER 1

Marriage: When Divorce is Not the Answer

Forgiveness---Communication---Teamwork---Restoration

DIVORCE

Carolyn:

Divorce is a tool to get released from a covenant between two people if there is a breach or breaking of values. Divorce is such an ugly word. There is nothing pleasant in the break up, the separation, or the emotional, spiritual and even sometimes physical pain. Divorce is like a death. You've gotten used to living with a person, sleeping with a person, eating with a person, trusting a person, vacationing with a person, going to church with a person, attending school recitals with a person, hoping dreams and destinies will be fulfilled with that person. Then suddenly, they are gone. It's over. It's done.

Usually divorce is grieved just like a death. The marriage is dead and over, but unlike a death you still have to communicate with this person... especially when there are kids involved. You will be communicating throughout your children's lives; from school, to college, from weddings to grandchildren. It is never ending and inevitably a part of your life.

Thomas:

Also, when comparing divorce to death, I am reminded of how your everyday routine changes. There was no morning kiss from the wife, no good morning daddy from the kids, it was all gone overnight. Having lost my father in 1990 was the same way. No time with him visiting, calling or just being there. My dad was gone and now my family was gone. Yes, they are still alive, but not accessible in the same way as I knew them before. When I got the papers resolving the divorce as final, I was numb. I didn't know how to react. Just like in the loss of a loved one, people try to encourage you but nothing stops the pain. So, in rare form I chose to drop my restoration, my sanity and my hopes by using again. Thankfully while at work I heard a message on the radio about King David recovering all. I will share more about this later. I decided it wasn't over until God says it is over. The court had spoken, but so had my faithful, loving, Father God!

God didn't create divorce but He allows it. We as people make decisions based on emotions. This blurs our vision on what we really have. So divorce allows us to break the contract and disavow the covenant. Sometimes it may be necessary but it is not always the answer. When Carolyn asked God if she should divorce me, God said I am with you if you do and I am with you if you don't. This proves God's word is true. Carolyn's heart had been hardened after so much pain, distrust and disappointment that God was willing to allow her to be released from the marriage. As people of God we need to keep our hearts open to receive instructions in difficult situations. God knew that Carolyn loved Him, obeyed Him and trusted Him, so He was gentle with her in bringing her to the place where He could instruct her to reconnect. Keeping God first will always get you in the right position.

Matthew 19:8 says, "He saith unto them, Moses because of the hardness of your hearts suffered you to put away your wives: but from the beginning it was not so." (KJV)

Having been the one that broke the contract I had to begin by accepting the consequences of my actions. Did the consequences hurt? Yes! Were they shameful? Yes! It opened the door to things that would only increase that negativity. I lost it all, my family, my position in ministry, my health, and my dreams. Even though people tried to encourage me, divorce led me to an empty life.

I wanted to blame my situation on drug abuse. No matter how much my mind said "I love my wife, my family, and ministry," I had proven that I did not love myself. Drug addiction is a slow form of suicide. It kills, tears relationships apart, destroys integrity, and causes you to be repulsive and to lower any standards you may have thought you had. One thing is for sure, as long as you are addicted, the destruction never stops. Drug addiction's biggest asset is its deception. Many seem to be able to handle it and function. But it does not care how long it takes to destroy you just as long as you stay in the process. Addiction is actually a form of adultery; spiritual, mental, emotional, physical and it even affects your imagination. It pulls you to choose the results of feelings over any and everything that is dear to you. Its main focus is to get you to risk all.

After watching the disintegration of my life and everything I loved, like the prodigal son I came to myself. The only question I had was, "Is it too late to recover all?" I can't speak for everyone or every situation, but I will speak for mine. I asked God a question: "If I go after all I had lost could I recover it?" While at work one night, I heard on a radio program the story of David in I Samuel 30 where he and his men had lost their families and their possessions to an enemy that had always been a problem for Israel. The narrator said that although they had lost everything, no one was killed, which signaled a sign of hope for recovery. David and his men wept, cried, then became angry and blamed David for their loss. David was encouraged because he knew he could turn to the Lord. "And David enquired at the Lord, saying, Shall I pursue after this troop? shall I overtake them? And he answered him, Pursue: for thou shalt surely overtake them, and without fail recover all." (I Samuel 30:8) That encouraged me that I would overtake, overthrow, overpower and overcome drug addiction, and without fail recover all.

Carolyn:

The day I went to court to finalize the divorce was the day I realized I was going to be a single mother. I felt like it was over. I had been through so much, now it had come to an end. After eleven years of dealing with his drug abuse, it was all over. I thought maybe I will take myself to lunch at my favorite Chinese restaurant. No wait, I deserve to go shopping, I deserve it all! Lunch, shopping, a mani/pedi... then it hit me; I needed to go home, relax and prepare for my kids to come home from school because life as they knew it was over. Any hopes and dreams they might have had of the family being together was over!

Now the death of the marriage has begun. This is what I call the Year of Firsts. The first birthday, Christmas, Easter, summer holiday, vacation, and concerts for the kids without their dad. Thomas was not around to celebrate any holidays or birthdays, or attend any concerts, et cetera the first year after our divorce. Although it was painful, at this point, I knew my kids and I had to depend on God and keep moving. There is life after divorce, but as a family, we had to initially deal with the pains of these firsts. Thankfully we got through the pain of life being different than the norm, through the personal heartbreak of experiencing a failed marriage even after I did everything to try and save it; through the sheer pain of having drugs be "the other woman." Of course, there was a feeling of abandonment, left alone to raise kids and make sure the finances earned would cover the needs and desires of the family. The death of my marriage left me with a feeling of embarrassment, not just for me but also for my kids. Simply because we were known before as a "great example of family" in the church and community.

With divorce usually comes a time to grieve. No one knows how long that grieving period is but you. At some point you have to get up and say okay, now I am ready to do this. For me, it was after the Year of Firsts. I had to allow God to heal me and my kids so I could say okay, God let's do this! Did I still have moments of crying, feeling alone and struggling with my kids' emotions? Yes. But when I made up my mind and knew I was going to have to get up and get going because there is life after divorce, everything came together. I found an excellent job with great benefits, paying more than any job I had previously. I purchased a new home and travelled. I was given a car and ultimately became more confident in myself. I began to enjoy my new life with a peace I cannot explain. I received total healing and forgiveness from God. Through counseling my kids understood they were not from a dysfunctional family but lived with only one parent and functioned as a healthy family. In counseling they were able to look around the room, see their peers and get the support they needed from them to create a sense of normalcy, to the point that they wanted to participate in after school activities. I believe counseling helped my children function throughout the day at school and gave them encouragement that they could get through this time.

Divorce is a roller coaster of emotions. You're up one day and down the next, hating the other person one minute, then feeling sorry for them the next. Not to mention the sorrow you feel for the kids. When will I be normal? Normal is what you make it. But you do not understand my situation! Yes, I do! You can stay in the situation the way it is, or you can decide to change it. Even if you are at peace and everything is going wonderful, there is still room for change.

As for children, they will adjust to change quicker than you think. Life can be better with the right words of encouragement, love, support and patience. Kids do have feelings and emotions which can manifest through their actions. I would not say anything negative in front of my kids regarding their dad. Instead I would encourage them to call and write their dad. My children were taught that the only dad who will not let you down is Daddy God. By me being understanding, listening and giving them support, they appreciated me even more.

Thomas:

Counseling played a huge part in my restoration. There was always someone who was willing to believe God for me. I stayed at several homes of people who were called to Paraclete (those who walk alongside those who need a push). These people offered Bible studies, meetings, housing, food, transportation and job opportunities. I eventually ended up staying at the rescue mission in Holland, Michigan which is about thirty miles from where my family was still living in Grand Haven, Michigan. After I started doing well again, not using, attending church and staying in touch with my kids, doors began to open for me, a ram in the bush so to speak.

So, counseling gave me the hope and faith push to try again and not give up. Twenty years later I am providing the same resources that was given to me; counseling, food, hope, shelter, and most of all faith pushes to walk alongside those who have a need.

FORGIVENESS

Forgiveness is the intentional and voluntary process by which a victim undergoes a change in feelings and attitude regarding an offense. Let go of negative emotions such as revenge, with an increased ability to wish the offender well.

The idea of having to forgive someone for the wrong done to you can be so scary. You know that forgiving is right, but you want to hate a little longer, remember what was done to you a little longer, stay mad forever. But you know in order for you to be free and move on, forgiveness is a part of the process. By embracing and receiving forgiveness you can also receive peace, hope, gratitude, joy and freedom.

Ephesians 4:32 says, "And be ye kind one to another, tenderhearted, forgiving one another, even as God for Christ's sake hath forgiven you." (KJV)

Carolyn:

I can remember when I started to realize if I wanted to go on with life, then I had to forgive. I had the new home, great job, and great kids. But the one ingredient for me was to be free in my soul, spirit and mind. It was hard because I had poured my life into this marriage. I had done everything in my power (marriage conferences, marriage counseling, get-aways, etc.) to keep our marriage together. Yet I had to forgive him! I knew this was right, but I was not ready. Funny how you know something is right, but you do not want to do it even though you know it will bring peace and joy. I had consciously made up my mind to do this! So, I started to think of my then ex-husband as a person that is dying within himself. This is the father of my children. Suppose he died? That would be horrible for them to live without a father. Who would give them away at their wedding? They would have a horrible story to tell their kids and my sons would have to look for leadership examples outside of the home. So, I began to pray that God would bring him to himself. That God would have mercy on his life; that he would live and not die! Then I had to say these words, "I forgive him, and I release him."

Wow, my heart was breaking for me. I did not want to forgive him, stop hating him, or stop wishing something bad would happen to him. It took months for me to convince myself that I had to forgive him and to pray for him every time I thought wrong of him. I do believe that my prayers were part of the reason that he came to himself. I was sincere with praying, but still had to be convinced of the forgiveness. Then one day it happened, I woke up and I felt strange.

Now this happened after a couple of years and a couple of months. After I decided I could be a single parent and could do this, then there was peace within my heart. I was like wait, what is this weird feeling? My head was clear. No crazy thoughts, no wondering about what if, just this peace that I could not understand. I waited for a week, still the same feeling; okay two weeks, still the same, one month, still the same. I decided this really feels good. A couple of months went by and then a couple more months went by again. Then it hit me, this is real forgiveness. I know my kids could see a difference in my attitude because I could see the difference. I felt much lighter and not bogged down. Things began to look brighter. I began to dream again. I wanted to change things from rearranging furniture and getting a new job, to buying something new. I felt it was time for change; it was time for increase, time to settle in with my family and enjoy life. It was time to even be ready to receive forgiveness and be able to forgive. I couldn't have done this in the first year; I had to work through my emotions first.

Emotions of feeling alone, abandonment, unforgiveness and not knowing if the peace of

God would be there. Praying daily, listening to my Christian music and surrounding myself with people who really wanted me to succeed helped me get through my feelings of pain, hurt, unforgiveness and abandonment. I had confidence in God and myself that I would be okay and with Him, I could do this!

There is nothing like freedom. I knew I was set free from the past with him and willing to deal with my emotions so I could move on with my life, my dreams, and my children's dreams and desires. I did not want to take this heaviness with me into another relationship, but I wanted to live a happier and healthier life and love myself so I could fulfill my dreams and desires.

To this day, I still have that feeling of freedom and it feels great! Forgiveness has taught me that I have control over me and no one else. In order for me to succeed in life I had to learn to forgive family, friends and associates because people will let you down and try to destroy you and your dreams. In order to go on and push through, forgiveness is needed. That has been a huge lesson for me. It is not always easy, but the results are great. I can say a benefit of forgiveness is peace, joy, freedom and a wealthier and healthier life.

Thomas:

Forgiveness first comes when there is an admission of doing, saying, or even believing something is wrong - even if you think it is right. I had to admit I liked getting high! Yes, I enjoyed it. I liked the escape it provided from anything that made me be accountable to and for my life's situation. I knew how to look successful, talk professionally, dress according to whatever situation it called for and even cover up my weaknesses.

I spoke earlier about how I came to myself. I had begun the process of restoration in my personal life by returning to what was right. Not what I thought was right, but what was right. During this time, I was challenged to return to the place of escape whether I was looking for drugs or not. As I forgave myself for all the mess I created, my enemy had begun to lose power over my decision-making process. One day I was driving and saw a former companion still caught in the web. I thought, "Wow, I can get with them, get high and continue as if nothing ever happened." This time that thought was countered by a consciousness of what it would really be like after the choice to return to my enemy. I saw the despair, separation, shame and recovery process starting over. I rode by them and to this day they never knew I saw them. Also, to this day I have never returned to that enemy. That was nineteen years ago. I had been forgiven, was living for myself and accepting the life that was being rebuilt without my wife.

To forgive does not mean to forget. It means it is not counted against you. There are definitely consequences that come with bad choices. I didn't deserve my family back, to be restored to ministry or the opportunity to rebuild my character. But with forgiveness came grace. The true heart that was in me was exposed and it broke down barriers that only God could break. God uncovered the Thomas He meant me to be; His son, my children's father, my mother's beloved son, a man with the heart of a Pastor who was ready to share his life with those who fought the same enemy and yes, my wife's new husband. God opened the door for communication.

Forgiving yourself is definitely a process that takes time, sincerity, truthfulness and allowing your heart to be mended. I didn't really think much of myself. I had always felt inferior for some reason. My parents and brother always loved me, but all I saw was rejection. I compared myself to others too much. I only saw my weaknesses, not any strengths. I know now that low self-esteem was behind it. It doesn't matter where it came from, it was a lie.

When I had the love of a wife, children and family in abundance I couldn't receive it. Instead

I did everything to destroy it, but my family never gave up on me. Were they disappointed? Yes! Broken hearted? Yes! Ashamed? Yes! They had to watch me destroy myself, but they refused to stop loving me! I was able to forgive myself because of God's hand and grace on my family. I saw the effects of Jesus giving His life in my family's heart toward me. I can now remember looking in my mother and father's eyes, my brother's eyes, my children's eyes and even my wife's eyes and seeing the heartache. Thankfully, I'm past that; the love of God shined through. I'm forgiven and I receive it!

COMMUNICATION

Communication is basically talking to someone and letting them know your thoughts, your belief, your story and your reason why. When you communicate it is your responsibility to let the person you are talking to know what you are communicating. Communication comes through voice, gestures, and motions.

Carolyn:

Before we got married, it was not communicated to me that Thomas had a drug addiction. We went on dates and he was the perfect gentlemen (opening and closing doors, paying for everything, buying nice gifts, holding intelligent conversations, etc.). We talked about marriage, he had his job and I had my job. We did not live together before marriage, we did not put our money together, and he did not abuse me verbally or physically. He spent time with my son (before we married, I had a son and he had a son and daughter from previous relationships). But somewhere I was not reading those hidden signs that should have indicated there was a problem. Although others may have known, they did not share it with me. I had no idea until after we were married and it was communicated through actions - money missing, people looking for him, shortage of funds to pay the bills or purchase food, him staying out late with friends and me having to listen to family members express our marriage was a mistake. By this time, I am thinking there has to be another women for sure. No way did I think he was having a love affair with drugs.

Communication is a vital part of any relationship whether it be with your spouse, children, boss, Spiritual Leaders, God, friends, etc. The thing about communication is that trust is a factor. Sometimes there is a lack of communication in some areas because there is a lack of trust. We could talk about church, friends, jobs, and finances before marriage, but could not talk about his addiction. Was he fearful I would leave? Was he trying to change and eliminate his addiction so we would not have to have the conversation? I believe it was both. This was his moment to try and change. Now that he has a family, dreams to fulfill, an opportunity to let others know he has taken on a new life and is a new person. I often asked myself what I would have done if I knew he had a drug addiction before we got married. I WOULD HAVE RUN! Once we were married, I saw the "real" Thomas; the minister, loving husband and father, I saw a different person and he was trying to change so I decided to stick it out. Within those eleven years he would go two to three years with no drugs or alcohol, and then the cycle would begin again. Why couldn't he communicate he had the urge to use again? Was it because he did not trust me or did, he just like getting high and chose not to communicate it?

There are times in a relationship where you need to communicate about the birds, trees, weather, and just those little things. To keep a relationship fresh, it is not important to always talk about "the deep things." Sometimes when I am with friends, we decide we are not talking about kids, husbands, work, church, etc. So, what do we talk about? Our business plans, TV programs, a pair of shoes or dress spotted in the window while shopping, a book we are reading, magazines, recipes, etc. It's just a good time of laughter and fun and my how time flies! Simple talk with no hidden agenda does the heart and soul good.

Communication starts at the beginning of your day and continues even when you're asleep. Even dreaming is a form of communication. You cannot live without communication. It has to be decided how far you will go and what is important. Whether dating, married or just getting to know someone, you need to communicate the real you because if you don't, eventually "you" will show up and it might be too late to save the relationship.

If Thomas would have communicated, I could have helped him... if he wanted help. I would have understood the reason behind the craziness instead of drawing my own conclusions. Communication would have also stopped all the lies.

It might be painful, it might hurt you, and you may be taking a risk, but communication is the key! Now we have a great marriage. We understand each other's gestures, moods and even what the other is thinking. We attribute it all to communication. Now we purposely take time to talk, even about challenges we might be having and our true feelings. That brings so much freedom to the relationship. Nothing is too small or too big to talk about. It is an investment that is worth taking the risk.

Thomas:

Have you heard the saying, "What's done in the dark eventually comes to the light?" Well not communicating with your spouse or others allows darkness or issues to only have power over you when it's not brought to the light. My lack of communication of my struggle with drugs made Carolyn feel powerless and vulnerable to the hazards and dangers that drug culture brings. Sometimes we are afraid we will lose things if we are too open or we actually think we can take care of it alone. Whatever we feel or think, when others' safety and happiness are involved, they should have the opportunity to help or walk away so you can take care of the problem. Either way communication early is better than later. Your spouse should be your biggest supporter not your biggest threat. To be able to communicate with your spouse takes courage. The biggest threat against communication is timing. We think there is a certain time we should share certain information. But there are issues where time needs to be made and not waited on to share with your spouse and others.

There were things Carolyn wanted to share with me, but when she was ready to share my struggles came to overshadow what she was dealing with which in turn caused a greater communication gap. When waiting on a perfect time to communicate essential information, make time because the sooner the issues are brought into the light, they lose their power to hurt and even destroy what has been built.

For Carolyn and me we try not to wait for a perfect time, we make time. Tell your spouse you need to talk so the time can be made to get any issue resolved which will bring more strength, power and most of all trust to your relationship. I'm reminded of a Pastor's quote, "Are you sharing the details of your devastation or your deliverance?" (Steven Furtick)

I want to speak about my drug addiction. I was not true to myself or my family. I portrayed someone who was really trying to quit, but in reality, my selfish desires were first in my life. The choices were mine to make so I communicated a lie. I cried, I asked "What's wrong with me?" I did everything but face my reality. I was selfish. When I came to myself, I was able to communicate the truth. I put the things that were supposed to be first by changing my attitude and taking responsibility for my actions. I was able to make the decision to be free.

God allowed me to be delivered from all the things that were first in my life that were of no use, value or benefit. When I changed, my communication changed! My family saw the ME

God had created. My point in all this is to be true to yourself and you will communicate sincerity, love and appreciation for the things that matter most. God, family and self!

TEAMWORK

Teamwork - Cooperative work by a group or work produced by a group or team. Cooperation, Collaboration, Joint effort. Teamwork is done on several associations with each doing a part but all subordinating-personal prominence to the efficiency of the whole. Cooperative or coordinated effort on the part of a group of acting together as a team in the interests of a common cause. (Wikipedia)

There is no "I" in Teamwork. It takes cooperation, effort, trust and of course more than one person. When you work as a team you need to have a goal. Even in marriage you should always have short-term and long-term goals for yourself and your family. You should always work toward a goal that is best for the family.

Before the divorce we always worked together to have the best for our family. It took us to operate as a team to make sure the best was done for our family. We supported each other with decisions that were made, and we might not have always agreed but we did what was best for the team. We decided where we would live, how our children would be raised and disciplined; we agreed on the rules for our household, rules concerning our family members, finances, intimacy and friends. If it did not fit in our plan, it was not a good fit for our team. One thing about being a team (even though things can be difficult, and you do not always agree) the team has to know you have its best interest in mind.

There can only be one leader and one co-leader, everyone else follows, but you take in consideration the feelings of the team and respect all the team members. Treat them right but remember what is best for the team is the main goal.

We had family meetings before and after the divorce. Even now we still have meetings, even though we are in different states (thank God for technology). We update each other throughout the year. We discuss situations in our family and our goals for the upcoming year, record them and each person gets a copy of what was discussed. Through the year we will pray, believe and hold the person accountable to complete their goals. During and after the divorce it was important to continue the meetings because this was the norm for our household and it still gave the children a sense of family and an outlet. We would meet once a week and it gave the family the opportunity to discuss things about school, home,

and church. The first year of the divorce our meetings were about getting things in order in our home, Bible study, and dealing with emotions of being afraid, why their daddy was not home and if he still loved them. So, I would encourage Thomas to make sure to keep in contact with the children to reassure them of his love for them and that even though he was not in the home he is still there for them. In our meetings, if things came up where they needed his encouragement or input as their dad, I would let him know. After our meetings we would sometimes watch a movie or even play a game which afforded us more family time. These family meetings lasted until our last child went to college. Life is so busy that we can forget about the small things, but when you pull together as a team, everyone has their own responsibility which makes it less stressful. We all have a part to play. Everyone just has to know their role. Keep in mind what is best for the team (family). Teamwork makes the dream work!

RESTORATION

Restoration - The act or process of retaining something to its original condition by repairing it, cleaning it. The act of bringing back something that existed before. The act of returning something that was stolen or taken. (Merriam Webster Dictionary)

Carolyn:

Forgiveness, communication and teamwork are intricate parts of the process of restoration. They start the act of restoring something to its original condition. That condition for us is marriage. Not the first marriage we created but taking this marriage to its original intent which is that of a true union. Knowing that you have to forgive the person and you lets you know you are ready to move on. Whether you decide to restore or move on, forgiveness is necessary for you to be free.

Communication opens the door to discover the other person's dreams, desires and plans for the family. When we were not together, we had to learn to communicate for the sake of our children. But when it came to us being restored, I had to learn more about his plans. Besides he was getting ready to be the leader in our home again. What were his plans for the family now that he was back? What was his plan of restoration? In this process we began to hear the others' desires, plans and even how we wanted our family to be successful. When being restored it is important to really hear others' thoughts, plans and mindset to be able to communicate your true feelings. You do not want to bring old baggage into something new. So, you have to talk a new talk and walk a new walk to be unchained from the past.

Teamwork is working together to be restored. It is not just my way or his way, but it is the best way for the household. Have a plan to work together with the result of restoration in mind. Once you have been restored, it is time to put another plan in place. It takes work. We continue to work on everything from talking about sex to housework. We have a plan even as empty nesters so it is not all on one person. We work together to keep the family functional.

Restoration is a place of happiness, peace and joy. If you want to be restored to the original condition for any other reason, it will not work. Being restored for just status quo will not work. Restoration brings a state of completeness and assurance that everything is in its proper place. You cannot start the process unless you trust and believe everything is going to be okay. Don't give up even if you do not get the response you are expecting. You have to remember restoration is continual; it is an ongoing process. I used these steps:

1. I started meditating on God's Word and after that I knew I was ready to remarry.
2. I observed Tom's behavior toward different situations and the kids.
3. I talked to my Pastor to get the right counsel.

4. I practiced patience to prepare and share my life with someone.

The guidelines we followed when we started dating were setting boundaries, learning to communicate, learning to be friends and to talk about everything no matter how large or small led to being remarried within one year on Thomas' birthday.

We are being restored to the original state every day because we are still taking the time to enjoy and learn each other. Even after a total of thirty-one years of being together, he still makes me laugh, puts a smile on my face when I think about him, opens my door, holds my hand and talks with me about everything.

Restoration is a process. We have shared four areas of our journey to a successful remarriage. Divorce, forgiveness, communication and teamwork led us to restoration; the final leg of the process.

To restore means to mend or put back to its original state. The way it should be. In our first marriage there were issues that were not addressed. As in many marriages people do not take time to deal with personal issues that may later cause problems and open the door to infidelity and place an undue burden on your spouse that may prove to be more than they can handle. To restore a marriage to its desired and blessed state these issues must be confronted and addressed.

Thomas:

For me, I had not dealt with a desire for drugs that led to an addiction I needed to confront. The amazing thing is that when I decided God, my life and family meant more than anything else, I was able to confront the addictions, as well as childish behavior, and man up so I could live a fruitful life.

One of the ways I dealt with the things that stood between my restoration and continual failure was to realize I had to submit to something. We, especially men, do not want anyone to rule over us. I found out that something or someone will always have authority over me. Sure I can make choices on my own, but that's the real issue. How was I making choices? Was it to fulfill my desires no matter the cost to myself and others or was it for my pride and ability to prove nobody was going to tell me what to do? I continued to say I love God, family, success and good health, but my actions proved different. That was pride! It is great to be proud of accomplishments. But at what cost? Was it helping or destroying my life?

During my restoration process, I was humbled and ridiculed for even believing I could get this woman to come back to a hell she got no benefit from. There were those who believed with me so I kept them close and avoided those who did not. I was on a mission to win. When I got serious about my decision to fight the battle against my enemy, I submitted to the process of restoration, no matter the cost. If it meant being alone, so be it. If it meant staying totally away from anything that could jeopardize my goal, so be it.

During my time of solitude, I was given a challenge by a friend. She said, "Do you really want your wife back?" I said, "Yes, I do." She responded, "ACT LIKE IT!" I took that challenge and declared that Carolyn was my wife period. When people said, "You're divorced." I would tell them, "Carolyn is divorced, I'm still married." I acted married in my actions. I did not approach her that way, but I approached life that way. My character said I am married. The way I handled my relationships with other women I worked with or ministered to said I was married. I was available to my family for whatever they needed. I sought no affection or physical relationship with Carolyn. I was praying one day and God said why are you talking to Carolyn about coming back to you? You can't convince her. No way no how. You should be talking to Me because she will listen to Me. I can soften her heart to receive My plan for both of you.

First God restored me to life, then to ministry, then to my family. As I submitted to His plan, I became the man she and my children not only wanted but needed in their lives as well as a man of God with purpose. My process of restoration was:

1. I tore down things that were built up in me to protect my choices no matter how destructive they were.

2. There was mending of the affected areas: mind, thoughts, attitude and character.

3. A repairing of my choice process.

4. A faith that I could and will recover all.

I Samuel 30 talks of King David losing his family, his warriors, their families and the respect as a man of God. He humbled himself, asked God could he overcome this devastation and got the answer that outweighted his adversaries' apparent victory. God said David, "You will recover all without fail!" I took that example of restoration and followed the process. Just like David, my family, ministry and physical health was restored.

CHAPTER 2

Ministry

Restoration is a Process

Carolyn's Perspective on Being Restored to Ministry:

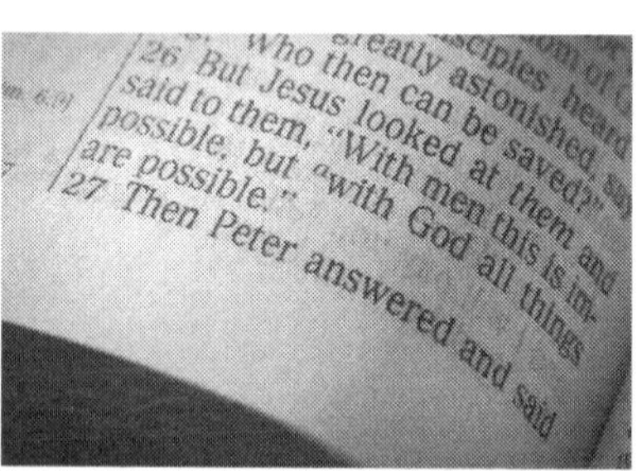

Ministry as I knew it was not the same. It included God, my husband and me, my family and church. Except my husband and I were no longer a couple in our church. The marriage ministry no longer existed for us. Being Associate Pastors no longer existed for us. But there were some things that did not change; me being the Treasurer, a Teacher of the Gospel and me being involved in Praise and Worship. I was given the responsibility to oversee the singers as well as leading the Prayer Group. As I continued these works, I realized my time was being demanded with a full-time job, raising my family and church.

Now you may think this is out of order that church would be first. But God was first! So I inquired, asked and sought God. What am I to do? My family needs me and the church needs me. God instructed me to sit back and began to spend time with my children. After I got home from work and attended meetings or went to work at the church, leaving my children at home was not a good move. One would think God might say you take care of My house and I will take care of your house. God ministered to me that I was a part of His house and that I could not take care of His house until my house was on a strong foundation. Experiencing divorce and having four children to raise, I needed to spend time with my children and build a strong foundation as a single mother.

I decided to relinquish all of my church responsibilities for six months to start my journey of building a strong foundation for my children and concentrate on being a single parent; which meant sitting with my kids and eating dinner with them, asking them about their day, attending recitals, basketball games, track meets and PTA meetings. This gave me the opportunity to reconnect with my kids all over again. We even had a time on Sunday when we would watch TV. We looked forward to the Sunday line up! We ate popcorn, laughed and just had a good old family time together. I know this paved the way for how close I am with my children today and even them still asking me life changing questions. I took classes on how to discipline and interact with my kids. This six-month process gave me the opportunity to start teaching them more about God. We went through every scripture of the Bible that talked about God as our Father. Of course, this took more than six months.

After one year, I began to take on some responsibilities at the church. At this time I was more careful of my decisions. I believe I was so involved and taking on so much in an effort to stay busy and ignore my hurt and anger. In reality, I was not allowing myself to be open and give God time to heal me. I also learned a lot about God being my Father and renewing my relationship to Him. So the study of Father God did us all some good.

As I was taking that break, I began to trust God as my Father like never before. While I was able to get a great job and buy a home and car, during this time God began to tell me that I was alone. I asked how that could be because I was so involved in my church and I had friends at work. God revealed to me those who said they were really for me did not have my best interest in mind. I started to see jealously, envy and even people who did not want my kids to be successful. So it was time to rethink and make a move.

There were some people I had to let go of but there were still those who wanted to see me get ahead and be a successful single woman. I knew the one place I could not leave was my church because God told me that my husband was coming. So I waited and I was restored as

Thomas' wife. While waiting, I had to believe God had my best interest and I really had to trust him. It was about two years after I heard God tell me that, then Thomas began to come around.

He was working in a church in Lansing, Michigan and I was living in Grand Haven, Michigan which is over 100 miles one way. God put it on the heart of the Teen Challenge program Pastor, where Thomas was the Outreach Pastor, to have my Pastor in Grand Haven come and speak at a church service. Needless to say, he wanted to take a team with him and I was on the team. That is when my kids spent the weekend with Thomas. Not so long after that, we began to talk and get re-acquainted and the rest is history.

After we remarried, we were appointed to come and help build a stronger leadership team at Lansing Teen Challenge. After going back-and-forth to Lansing to build that team, they asked me to become the Women's Director of the Women's Maternity Program, the only Teen

Challenge Program that accepted pregnant women. I accepted the position and we moved to Lansing. I thought what an honor to be in full-time ministry to be able to help women become better moms, women and leaders in their community. That position lasted over a year. I taught classes to men and women twice a week and also wrote a lifestyle class which allowed the students to be reintroduced to society after being in the program for a year. I taught them how to write resumes, interview and even how to budget money wisely. It was a great experience!

When that assignment was done, Thomas and I knew God wanted us to start a church. We began Family on the Shore Ministries in Grand Ledge, Michigan. We started in our apartment which we outgrew and moved into a room in a library. We knew we needed more ministry and guidance, so we became a part of an organization, Excellence In Ministry (EIM). There our lives began to change and we were taught how to use our faith on another level. After being connected with EIM for about a year, we decided we would join our ministry with that church and we became members. Since becoming members, we have been ordained ministers, assistant pastors, the directors of the Marriage Ministry and we also taught Lifestyle courses and Ministry in Training classes.

But things did not end there. We had to deal with Thomas' health, which has caused me to really use my faith on a daily basis not just when I am at church.

Thomas' Perspective on Being Restored to Ministry:

Before God restored my family, He restored me to Him and to ministry for His purpose. He actually used ministry to bring Carolyn back to me. Carolyn thought, "If God takes him back, builds him up, uses him mightily, trusts him again, maybe I can." Little did we know that God had plans for us that were not to be discarded because of my disobedience. As I look back over my restoration to ministry, I am humbled by the grace, favor and disciplines God allowed me to experience.

Delight thyself also in the Lord; and he shall give thee the desires of thine heart. Psalms 37:4 (KJV)

As I walked alone, hurt, shamed, destitute and most of all faced with the failure in God, I again came to the story of David at Ziklag. I shall overtake, overcome and without fail recover all. All means all in God. I didn't focus on ministry, I focused on relationship. I just wanted God to minster to me, hold, protect, and show me a reason to live. Jeremiah 29:11 was already working in my life. There was hope and a future waiting for me, if I would submit. I was empty without my family, but I caused the pain so I directed my attention to The One that could carry me and gave me a reason to live no matter what I was facing. His love. "I tried to quit life but I couldn't" is a quote that I kept close in mind. God was always there, always watching, and always loving me even though I broke His heart too. My restoration took about four years to complete. It wasn't overnight, it wasn't a given, it was God's purpose for me if I would love Him first.

In 1996-98 I had several opportunities to get it right. I moved to Montgomery, Alabama with a cousin who is a successful pastor. He believed in me and wanted me to start my life over, even if it was without my family. I would always have my kids, but my marriage was over. I began to preach again and I had not used in about a year. It seemed all was well, but in rare form I began to use again. Even after being blessed to see God's hand on my life, I was still empty. I even helped start ministries for young boys, titled "Save Our Seeds." God is real, but we can be fake.

My cousin (who is more like a brother) shared a thought with me. He said your problem is you are willing to "risk all" to escape reality. You say you are a coward, but you will get involved with the deadliest drug situations without fear!

I realized I was so untruthful to myself. I liked

being high. I chose it over everything that was dear to me. Then I heard God speak through a radio program while at work. He talked about David at Ziklag. I took that word, decided I was going to fight for all as opposed to just some. With the same dedication and tenacity, I used to get my fleshly desires, I would get my family, ministry and health back. I moved back to Michigan after destroying all that had been rebuilt. I received the final divorce papers and took the easy way out AGAIN... I used.

I returned broken again but wanting to try. Listen, restoration is a process. It's not overnight, it's not a quick fix. I had no staying power. I had to be restored right. While walking the streets of Holland, Michigan, I was the laughingstock of the drug culture. I did not belong but insisted on staying. As I was walking one day, I ran into an old friend. He invited me over to his house. When I got there, I found out he and another former user had started a ministry for men who were trying to get off drugs. He invited me to move in. I left my drug buddies and disappeared into a Christian environment. There was Bible study fellowship and an opportunity to get back to God. My kids were able to visit and I worked to regain life again. I will always remember these times. I still had not gotten back to ministry. As unbelievable as it may be, I still used again. I left the house, returned to the streets and proceeded to die; both naturally and spiritually.

It was Fall 1999 and I was on the streets using, going from day to day, just existing. I will never forget that day because it was my wife's birthday, October 1, 1999. I got up, and said I can't take this any longer, I'm done! I confessed I was done with the life I was destroying and chose the life God had for me. I called a friend, a pastor, who immediately told me if I was serious get to him and his ministry. It was fifty miles away! I called another friend who said if you are serious, I'll put you on a bus! I took the offer. My drug buddies asked if they could go, but I left them there. I had to do this alone, for me.

When I arrived at the ministry they received me with open arms, but with caution. You see I used to be their leader, their go to guy, their mentor. Now I had failed them, as well as everything I loved.

Their words to me were God wants to deliver you. This is between you and Him. We will give you shelter, food and structure for no charge, but you're on your own. It was a terribly lonely time, but a necessary one. I watched as the brothers were fellowshipping, laughing, praying and study God's Word without me. I was left to be restored by the only one who could, God!

You see I had become a bad testimony. Someone who ministered to hundreds about God and His grace while falling to my own weaknesses instead of allowing the love of Christ to work on my behalf. No one could get through to me, only God could fix this. And He did!

After a few months of prayer, study, devotion and just plain hard work God had shown himself to me again. I was lonely, empty and weak. I remember a fellow program director saying, “Tom, if you want your family back act like it. Stay away from the women and respect the situations of accountability.” I did just that. Soon I was asked to oversee a study session which led to teaching classes, going to the jails to share my story and the Gospel with lost and broken people. A local church had some of us working on a building and a pastor walked up to me and said, “Tom, you’re a minister, aren’t you?” He did not know me or my story. I was just another program student. I told him my story and he said, “God says you’re restored son.” I just said, “Thank you.” I knew who I was and was not about to take a single step without God himself saying let’s go.

I took a course called Cleansing Stream that ministered to the spirit, soul and body of a person. While in line for prayer, I was told to go to the line for pastors. I was very hesitant but obeyed. God moved mightily and from that day forward I have walked in my anointing by grace. I was ordained again, preached weekly, counseled men and women, oversaw a feeding and clothing program at a connected church and was mentored by that pastor daily. Now I was ready to see my children!

Carolyn saw my commitment and being the Woman of God, she is, she was not trying to keep my kids from me. She made sure I had a secure, safe, clean place to take them and brought them to see me. She even allowed them to spend weekends with me. It was so special to me. While being restored to the ministry, I was also given the opportunity to bond with my children. It was amazing.

Once Carolyn brought the kids to Lansing to spend the weekend with me, which was a great opportunity. The only problem was I was living at Teen Challenge, the Men's Center. It was not a problem for my son, Joseph who was six years old at the time, to stay there with me; however, it was not suitable for my girls, Jennifer who was fourteen and Charmaine who was thirteen. So, we had to come up with a plan. Carolyn respected Teen Challenge Ministry so much and trusted them, she agreed to allow the girls to sleep at our Women's Center under the care of the Women's Director and associate who challenged me to act like I wanted my wife back. We spent day and evening together shopping, eating, playing games, talking and helping me in the food pantry at the church where I was working. They enjoyed fixing food baskets, separating clothes and helping those who were less fortunate. They saw me operating in the office of a Pastor while putting them first in everything. At night, although the girls stayed at the Women's Center, I was able to read to them and pray over them before putting them to bed. As stated earlier, Joe and I went to the Men's Center to sleep and in the morning we would go to the Women's Center to get the girls and start our day all over again. This was a special time for us. These visits continued in Lansing and other weekend visits were arranged in Grand Haven.

This bonding time reinforced my desire to be back with them even more.

This was not a selfish gesture to get favor with Carolyn. I love my kids and missed them, all of them. But the hand of God is always in action when we work with Him. Carolyn being able to trust me with our young children was a major step in our restoration. If she could trust me with them her heart was not far behind. I began to have more time with my kids in Grand Haven, for example the Christmas of 2000 was the first time in four years I had spent with my children and Carolyn at her home. I was even allowed to visit them at the very church I was asked to leave and never come back (due to the terrible things I had done in my addiction).

It gets even better. My wife, her pastors and a ministry team were invited to minister at the very church I was working at through the program as a Pastor! She brought my kids and when they saw me leading service and walking in God's grace, it was so humbling. We spent time together as a family and they stayed for the weekend. God was not done yet.

Things seemed to be going great! I am spending time with the kids, Carolyn and I are friends, I am in ministry again! What could go wrong? Then it happened. The church and program I worked for as a pastor in Lansing, Michigan decided they were no longer going to partner with Teen Challenge and my services were not needed. This actually set me up for my transition back to Grand Haven. I was told I could continue living in the Men's Center, but they could not afford to pay me and I needed to get an outside job. I continued preaching, counseling and overseeing the food program as a volunteer. I must share that at the outside job I had I met an amazing couple that supported by efforts in my family being restored and to this day they are mentors to our life and our marriage. The leadership at the Men's Center began to transition and I was offered the opportunity to return working at the ministry full time as the Men's Center Outreach Pastor. But after five years of being divorced and separated from my children, I felt it was time to move on and decided to go back to Grand Haven to be close to my kids.

I called the Pastor of the church where my family attended, the same church I was told to leave and never come back (due to the terrible things I had done in my addiction), and asked if I could come back. I humbled myself and God moved again. I was told, "Sure, please come back because we need an associate pastor!"

After five years of being separated from my family and fighting to regain my life and going through the restoration process God ordained and put in place after the many disappointments I caused and endured, I was headed back home! Back to Grand Haven as a Pastor at the very church I was asked to leave and never come back!

A friend, whose son I mentored, offered me an apartment for no charge with everything I needed.

It was on ten acres of land. He continued to minister to me as a successful father, husband and man of God without a title.

Yes, I moved back restored, as a Pastor. Carolyn and I dated to be an example to others who wanted their marriage to work. After six months we were remarried on my birthday. Within two years we were ordained in Grand Haven, Michigan and moved to Lansing, Michigan because Carolyn was offered the position of Women's Director at Teen Challenge and also to start a church. During this process we visited a church there that was flourishing and decided to submit to the pastors as a covering for our church under their Excellence in Ministry Fellowship and our family became very connected. We continued having services at our church on Sunday mornings and attending their church on Sunday evenings. Our children became involved in their youth groups, dance and step team and Lifestyle classes.

While attending a service at that church an assistant pastor prophesied that there was someone who needed to stop what he was doing and get with what God was doing. I went to this assistant pastor and asked were you talking to me? He said something so profound. Look in your wife's and kids' eyes when they are here. When I looked in their eyes, I saw their joy and comfort. Little did I know that God was about to take Carolyn and I to a new level of Ministry.

Shortly after one year of having planted our church, Family on the Shore, that Carolyn and I started, we chose to shut it down and just be members at this awesome ministry. One day during a conference for pastors I was asked to be a doorman, opening doors for visitors. I wore a doorman jacket and hat! I accepted the task. God was about to blow me away! The pastor came to see how things were going, saw me, took a double take, but said nothing. I thought he would say, "Tom, you should not be doing this." He didn't say a word. As pastors arrived, I opened the door with a smile. “Whatever you want, Lord,” was my cry. I was humbled as they looked at me. Many pastors knew me and wondered if I had fallen AGAIN! Later that night something happened. While sitting in the back the Pastor called me and Carolyn to the front before more than thirty pastors and hundreds of church leaders. He said, “Tom, God told me to ordain you and your wife!” Restoration to ministry was complete!

We have been leaders over several departments such as School of Ministry and Lifestyle Courses. I preach to hundreds; counsel married couples and do whatever I am asked. To this day I am walking as a testimony of God’s restoration power.

CHAPTER 3
Health

Carolyn's Perspective:

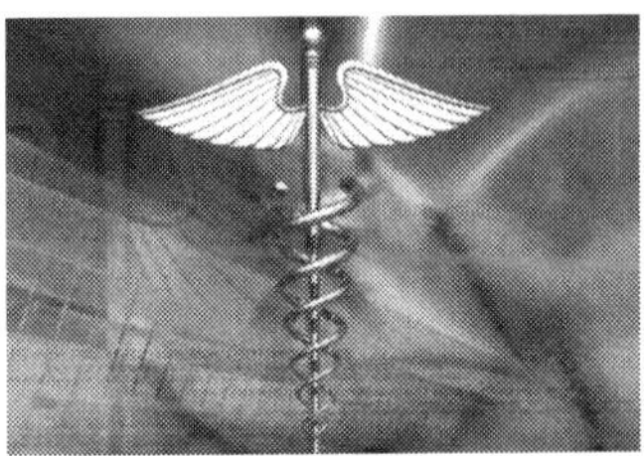

When I found out Thomas had Hepatitis C, I was not sure how I felt at first. I was not sure what that meant, if I would be infected or if it was contagious. So, I had to learn about it and how it would affect our living. Of course, you think it is like AIDS and then you begin to think the worst, but God has a way to turn things around.

After a couple of years of being married we continued to build our marriage and ministry. We began to notice that Thomas' legs were swelling. At that time we thought it was nothing and he just needed rest. In the meantime, he went for checkups and was told by the Gastrologist that he might need a liver transplant. He had seen this doctor previously and because of moving back to Grand Haven had lost touch with him. After we moved to Lansing, he saw him and he said I have been trying to find you to refer you to a Gastroenterologist (a physician with dedicated training and unique experience of the management of disease of the gastrointestinal tract and liver). God will use whoever is willing to be used to get the message to you.

Unknowing to us, our son (Joe) was friends with the doctor's son that was trying to find Thomas. One day while taking Joe's friend home, Thomas went to the door and his father immediately looked at him and said, "I have been trying to find you." He put two and two together and finally was able to be reacquainted with the doctor. We went to see the Gastroenterologist and he suggested a liver transplant and our lives started to change. God turned things around.

We visited the Transplant Center in Detroit, which was two hours from our home, and went through a series of appointments for Tom to get on the list. He was assigned a Transplant Coordinator and we had to take our family to meet them for the support we would need. We learned there was housing available across the street at the Henry Ford Hospital Campus, so we would be able to stay there after his transplant until he could go home.

He was told that if you do the things we tell you to do: do not smoke, do not drink alcohol, then you will be eligible for a liver transplant. Because of his obedience and keeping all his appointments, within thirty days God miraculously moved him from the bottom of the transplant list to being the first. This meant we had to stay ready because we could get the call to go to the hospital at any time. At that time we only told our immediate family and pastors because we wanted to make sure we continued in faith all the way until the end.

We received a call that there was a liver available and we had to be at the hospital within two hours. We packed up the car and headed to Detroit. After arriving at the hospital, Tom was prepped for the transplant. As we waited, it was around 5:00 am – we thought, "Praise God he would be done by 10:00 am." The doctor came in and said the liver was too fat to use, we had to go home. We packed up and headed back home. We continued to prepare and went back to work. Yes, Tom worked until the day he had the transplant!

Within the next month we received another call that a liver was available. Back to Detroit we went. He was prepped again and the surgery was scheduled for 4:00 am. Thank God, he will be transplanted by 9:00 am and on the way to recovery. Once again, the surgeon came and said the liver was too fatty. Thank God it was the weekend. We went back to work and continued to prepare, pray, fast and stayed in faith. Thank God the doctors wanted this transplant to be a success as much as we did and just did not use any liver that was not right for Tom. There were times when his legs were so big that he had trouble standing, but he continued to work and serve in the ministry.

Wow, six months after Tom reconnected with the Gastroenterologist, two disqualified transplant attempts, and traveling two hours from Lansing to Detroit to make multiple doctor's appointments, it is now the Easter Season and Tom's mom, Dorothy Little (R.I.H.), was visiting us from Gary, Indiana. He did not tell her about the transplant because she would have been so worried about him. So we planned on taking her home, two weeks after her visit. We went to an appointment in Detroit and they told Tom he could take her home, but to come right back just in case a liver was available. We decided we would leave the next morning and so we did some shopping in Detroit to prepare for our church's annual Women's Conference. Well guess what happened while we were shopping... you already know. We got the call that a liver would be available and we needed to be at the hospital as soon as possible.

We went home, had to tell his mom we could not take her home and disclose Tom's current situation (his Hepatitis C and need for a liver transplant). It seems like a lot to tell her all at once, but just as we thought (whether here with us or at her own home) she started to worry, but was glad she was with us and able to go to Detroit.

Once at the hospital they prepped Tom again and explained that the transplant would be in the morning at 9:00 am. The doctors asked Tom if he was ready for his new liver and he said yes. The doctors then said see you when you wake up! It really was time. We called our Pastors and talked to them. They prayed and told him we will talk to you when you wake up. I kissed him and he was on his way to surgery.

The surgery was about five hours. As his mom and I waited in the lobby we both were nervous, but the peace of God comforted us as we prayed, said confessions, read the Bible, and spoke to my

Pastors. Finally, the doctor came out and said Tom was in recovery and would be in an ICU room soon.

When I saw him I was shocked. He looked well, he was talking and ready to eat. (They called him the poster child for the transplant). I said, "Thank You, Lord!" By the end of the day he had no tubes, just the monitor system. Our family was able to see him and we were very pleased with his recovery. He could be released in five days to go home.

All the doctors were pleased and agreed he was able to leave the hospital in five days. I remember the social worker came and asked if he wanted to apply for social security/disability we both looked at each other and said, "No," and she looked at me and said, "Are you sure," and I said, "Yes." He will be going back to work and she asked me "Does he take good care of you," and I said, "Yes he does." After that, we did not see her the remainder of his hospital stay. Tom was released from the hospital with one prescription which was the liver rejection medicine that makes sure the liver continues to function properly.

We were off eight weeks for his recovery. Thank God for our church family supporting us with prayer, food and visits during that time. Even our landlord was a blessing and lowered our rent during his recovery time. The recovery plan included doctor visits to Detroit, Michigan twice a week, then weekly, then once a month for the first year. I remember going to the visits seeing other transplant patients on the elevator. They would say two years since my transplant and another would say five years since my transplant. God was still building our faith and letting us know that everything is going to be alright. It has been nine years since Tom's transplant! Thank God!

Even though it has been nine years since his transplant, within that time the disease that caused the transplant was attacking his new liver.

With continued doctors' visits and the monitoring of the function of his liver, we received a call that there was a treatment for the disease and he would be a great candidate for the treatment.

(The Poster Child!)

Since we were told the disease started attacking his new liver we prayed, sowed seed that he would be totally healed from the disease. We wrote it on the back of every tithe and offering envelope and every special offering that Tom would be totally healed. We believed God and within six years into the transplant we got a call that there was a treatment available that could possibly cure Hepatitis C!

In the meantime, we moved to Florida and inquired about the treatment of the doctors there. We were told they were understaffed and could not take any new patients. The doctor recommended we go back to Michigan. We contacted the transplant team in Detroit and they immediately explained the treatment and also that there was a possibility Tom would be eligible for a study. They scheduled him for an appointment.

In August 2014 we went to Detroit and were prepared to be there for at least two months. At the appointment we were informed that he was ineligible for the study but qualified for the treatment. Thank God that the doctors in Detroit could monitor the treatment while we were in Florida with weekly blood work and direct communication with our Family Physician. On our way home to Florida we received a call from Detroit that the treatment would be delivered in two days by UPS. While the cost of this treatment was supposed to be $12,000, Tom's cost was $135! Praise God!

Within four to six weeks of treatment, his body had to adjust to the treatment medications and his regular medicines. After the treatment was done, now it was time for the test results:

- First viral test - 09/23/14 –

Result: no detection of disease

- Second viral test - 11/17/14 –

Result: no detection of disease

- Third viral test - 12/2014 –

Result: no detection of disease

- Fourth and final test - 2/17/15 -

Result: no detection of disease

Thank God! Thomas is completely healed from Hepatitis C and his body is learning to live without the virus which meant that other tests and medications had to be adjusted! To God be the Glory, He turned it! Our marriage, our ministry and his health. We are enjoying the good life!

Thomas' Perspective: He Turned It... Health

It is amazing how so many areas of my life were affected by my decisions. We overlook, ignore, take for granted, and just plain don't respect our bodies as we should. At least I didn't. This is where I learned that choices have consequences, whether they are positive or negative. I felt like the Apostle Peter, who in the gospel of John 18:17 – "Then saith the damsel that kept the door unto Peter, Art not thou also one of this man's disciples? He saith, I am not." (KJV) He chose to deny Him. He did not have to, but because he did the consequences were shame, fear and degradation. Peter felt like everything they had worked so hard for was not only lost but over... Choices and Consequences.

Then in Acts 2:14 – "But Peter, standing up with the eleven, lifted up his voice, and said unto them, Ye men of Judaea, and all ye that dwell at Jerusalem, be this known unto you, and hearken to my words." (KJV) We see this same man but with a different heart, a different spirit; a man willing to choose faith over fear, stand up and not only confess he knows Jesus but that He is alive. Over 3,000 people accepted Jesus as their Savior! Choices determine Consequences.

After years of abuse and flagrant disregard for life, I began to see a pattern of health issues surface. To begin with I was a premature baby, three months early to be exact, two pounds and some change, an African-American male born in Memphis, Tennessee in 1950. Not exactly a healthy start. It was a different time for Blacks in the South. God favored me and I lived and grew strong. Even though I was frail in size, I was blessed. I didn't return to a hospital until I began working there as a teen in Chicago, Illinois. Life had been kind.

At seventeen years old, in my infinite wisdom, I decided being cool and following the crowd was what I wanted. This led to an almost thirty year off and on cycle of alcohol abuse and drug addiction. I already dealt with how my addiction led to my marriage and ministry being affected. Now I want to share how God restored my health from the consequences of my poor choices.

It is amazing how my deliverance from illness started the same time as my restoration for marriage and ministry. I was diagnosed with Hepatitis C while living in Lansing. I was told by my primary doctor that my liver enzymes were very elevated. We began to see a gastroenterologist and I was told there was no cure for Hepatitis C. I continued to see doctors and after Carolyn and I were remarried (in Grand Haven), I continued to be monitored closely. We moved from Grand Haven to Lansing and began seeing a new primary doctor.

Here is where it gets interesting. I was sent to a Gastroenterologist that had the same name as my previous one. When I saw the new doctor, I thought he looked different, but I just wanted help. My blood tests showed an increased viral load that wasn't looking good. We continued to believe God would move on my behalf and my wife's faith and support were phenomenal to say the least. She kept my spirits up, spoke healing continually, and loved me unconditionally. We never involved the kids with this challenge.

After a few years later, in 2008 to be exact, I ran into my first Gastroenterologist. He said, "I've been looking for you!" I made an appointment and he revealed that the virus had taken a toll on my liver. He said you need a liver transplant. Now a treatment had been developed that had some success, only it did not perform well with African-Americans. That meant me! A transplant seemed to be my only hope.

I'll never forget that day, my heart dropped into my stomach, I was numb, could not move and was at a loss for words. Then my Doctor said, "You'll be fine. I'm sending you to Henry Ford Hospital in Detroit because they're like Avis car rental, 'They try harder'," and they did!

Getting an organ transplant should be a long process. It could take years to find a match, and then its availability is determined by need. I was still working, strong and did not have extreme symptoms like the inability to think, loss or ability to care for myself, etc. I did have a lot of swelling in my lower extremities and stomach. I also was losing weight in my face and upper body. I remember a pastor's wife coming into my store and being overwhelmed by my appearance. She said, "Oh my God! Are you ok? You've lost so much weight!" I had no idea how much this disease had affected me. I was so used to grinding, working, ministering and keeping up with my kids that I just blocked it out.

I went to Henry Ford for an evaluation and they determined a transplant was necessary. About this time an associate pastor and I were talking and he told me about a pastor who was healed of Hepatitis C! Casey Treat was his name and he was a world known Pastor who had released a DVD on his process and healing. I sent for the DVD and watched it over and over. His determination to be healed by faith really encouraged me. Yes he took the treatment, chemo, and did everything the doctors advised. But most important he allowed God to use others to help him. One of his elders was a doctor that shared a scripture with him. Now remember Pastor Casey told no one except his wife and this elder. He wanted only those who were strong in faith involved. Sometimes you have to go it alone till you get things in order.

This elder gave him a scripture that I also embraced immediately. Proverbs 18:9, "He who is loose and slack in his work is brother to him who is a destroyer and he who does not use his endeavors to heal himself is brother to him who commits suicide." (AMPC) I repeated the scripture over and over and decided I must do something. Faith without works is dead. Could God touch me and my liver be healed? Yes! Could God just say be healed and I would be? Yes! But faith without works is dead. Sure I didn't want to go through this ordeal, but I thanked God for the option!

I began the process of being put on the list for a transplant. Remember, I am still working, preaching, teaching and dealing with the disease's side affects which were fatigue, a lot of swelling in my abdomen, legs and ankles. I often had to wear constrictive socks to decrease the swelling. I was unable to stand for long periods of time, found myself agitated easily and using the bathroom often. There were times, even though I pressed through the anxieties, I got depressed. That is when I quoted Proverbs 18:9 throughout the day and night to remind myself to use every endeavor to be healed, "He who is loose and slack in his work is brother to him who is a destroyer and he who does not use his endeavors to heal himself is brother to him who commits suicide." (AMPC) God was guiding me, comforting me and most of all being my encouragement! I did whatever the doctors prescribed. I made every appointment, took every test, did all I could and watched God move. We have heard faith without works is dead. I believed God could heal me anyway He chose.

Because I had been taught strong faith principles, I did not just look for a miracle, I acted like a miracle in progress. I had been down this road before. Remember I had my marriage and family restored after five years of divorce. I knew what God was capable of in my life so I acted healed even though the evidence was clear I was not that well.

My conversation, attitude and countenance spoke healing not sick and definitely not death. Kind of like the story of the Shunammite woman in 2 Kings 4:8-37 who was blessed with a son by God through the prophet, Elisha. Her son fell sick and died so she traveled to meet with the prophet. When asked how are you, your husband, and your son. She replied "IT IS WELL" even though her heart was broken at the loss of her son. She still declared IT IS WELL because she believed God would take care of this and if you read these verses you'll see the amazing power of faith at work.

This was in February of 2008 and my transplant coordinator told me I was NUMBER 1 on the list, after thirty days! This was a miracle, there were others who were much sicker, weaker, and who seemed to be at the end of their life, but I was number one on the list! Because many transplant patients do not go to their appointments, follow instructions and some even continue to drink alcohol and use drugs which I had not done for years!

For the next three months I had three false alarms. I was actually on the operating table once and the surgeon decided the liver was not perfect enough so he sent me home. I received several calls to be ready. We lived out of a suitcase because I had to be ready in a moment's notice. Time was of the essence.

I continued to thank God and in May of 2008 while shopping with my wife, I received the call we had been waiting for. It was time! Carolyn and I went home packed, got my mother and my brother would bring our kids and meet us there. My pastor prayed for me as I was headed into surgery and said, "I will talk to you after surgery and we look forward to seeing you when you get home." He only spoke faith. It definitely encouraged me as my family and I faced this surgery to save my life. My wife and mom were both with me.

On May 14, 2008, I received my new liver. As I lay on the operating table I remember the surgeon saying as the technician held up the new liver, "Are you ready for your new liver?" That was the last thing I remembered before I woke up and I was told it was a total success! My family came in, we thanked God for His goodness, grace, mercy and favor on my life while speaking blessings on the family that allowed their loved one's liver to be placed in me to save my life. I will always be grateful for their compassion and kindness.

I returned to work after only two months of rehabilitation and in my first month back I was featured in my company's newsletter for Sales Achievement. I said I would show my gratitude to the company by being the best sales representative I could since they stood behind me. God is awesome! He turned it! But the battle wasn't over. My challenges were not over. The hepatitis returned and began to attack my new liver. This was devastating. Would I need another transplant and how long before it would destroy my new liver? I turned to God and kept my faith. God did not restore my family and ministry for me to die happy, but for His purpose. I stood on that and did not question God. I kept going and after six years a treatment came out that was 85% successful. My transplant team got me on it right away.

This new treatment had proven to be positive for African-Americans as well as transplant patients. I was required to stay in Michigan for two months for monitoring, but I currently resided in Florida. It was ironic that the doctors in Florida told me about the treatment but could not take me as a patient! Carolyn and I had to take a leave from our jobs, set up provisions for my son who was attending college in Florida, and be prepared to stay in Michigan at a residence provided by the hospital. The cost for treatment alone was $12,000, not including housing. I had the opportunity to be a study patient. At least that would take care of the expenses, but when the blood tests were taken, I was informed I was not eligible for the study. I stayed in faith and my transplant team not only got me approved for the three- month treatment but allowed me to do the treatment in Florida.

Carolyn and I drove back to Florida from Michigan so very excited about the hope and opportunity to be healed. We listened to a song "He Turned It" from Indianapolis to Orlando declaring God's favor and purpose to be fulfilled.

While in route we received a call that the medicines would be delivered in two days! We drove 1500 miles non-stop! We were also told that the cost of the treatment was $12,000, but my cost was $135!!! God's grace is sufficient!

We returned home and began the treatment! I had to get blood tests every week to check my viral load, that is how much Hepatitis C was infecting my blood stream. After three months on this treatment there were minimal side effects. I returned to work, ministry and continued to get my results. Hepatitis C was not detectable in my body! I am clean!!! Glory to God!!!

I was so grateful of God's healing power through the treatment that I shared with others who had been diagnosed with Hepatitis C and now they are healed!!! Great ending right? Awesome right? Incredible right? Over? No!!!

God's not done yet and neither was my healing process. Right after this victory I am ready to live like never before. Carolyn and I started Lifestyle Soulutions, an Online Counseling Service. We were able to watch our son play college basketball, I preformed the marriage ceremony for two of my three daughters, witnessed my youngest daughter get her Master's Degree, and got the chance to hold my first granddaughter and see my sons raise awesome sons to be men and visit with my grandchildren. None of my offspring have a problem with drugs or alcohol!!!

All seemed well then I noticed the swelling again. The battle was not over yet!! The enemy was not giving up but neither was I, and neither was my God! Now I am reminded of what Jesus said to Peter in Luke 22:31, "And the Lord said, Simon, Simon, behold, Satan hath desired to have you, that he may sift you as wheat." (KJV) That means to shake you to the core, to break you down, to discredit your faith, actually he wants to make God look like a fraud! But Jesus came so we can have life and life more abundantly, even though the thief came to steal, kill and destroy (St. John 10:10). I declared I believe God is able, willing, and has healed me even though I am in the process!! Praise God!

Was my liver going bad, had the virus returned with a vengeance? I went to the doctor and found out a medication I was taking for my immune system started to affect my kidneys. My liver was fine. No Hepatitis detected, but now it's my kidneys. Am I overwhelmed? Do I think this is unfair? It does not matter. Can I handle this new challenge? I can do all things through Christ who strengthens me! Watch my God and I overcome this challenge as we have all the others.

God is turning everything around for me! I'm grateful to be able to share this awesome victory in my life. I have shared my testimony of how God healed me of Hepatitis C! I have shared that through all the adversity God has restored my marriage, ministry, and health and now I'm faced with another issue. Fear, shame and defeat seemed to be my inheritance, But God! I decided I would overcome this latest adversity the same way I have overcome my divorce, ministry and liver transplant and healing, by faith!!

Do not let anything stop you from believing God wants you healed, delivered and set free. Your entire life is important to Him. Jesus paid it all is not just a song, it's a reality, it's a promise, it's a blessing and it's the truth for you and for me!

Is this new challenge a promotion in the spirit? Jesus endured the cross bearing the shame for the joy that was on the other side. Promotion! Every knee will bow and every tongue will confess that Jesus Is Lord.

He Turned It!!! Hallelujah!

HEALING SCRIPTURES

These are the scriptures I used to build my faith and believe God for my healing!

Isaiah 53:4–5 (AMPC)

Surely He has borne our griefs (sicknesses, weaknesses, and distresses) and carried our sorrows and pains [of punishment], yet we [ignorantly] considered Him stricken, smitten, and afflicted by God [as if with leprosy]. But He was wounded for our transgressions, He was bruised for our guilt and iniquities; the chastisement [needful to obtain] peace and well-being for us was upon Him, and with the stripes [that wounded] Him we are healed and made whole.

ISAIAH 53:5 (NLT)

But He was pierced for our rebellion, crushed for our sins. He was beaten so we could be whole. He was whipped so we could be healed.

1 Peter 2:24

... who Himself bore our sins in His own body on the tree, that we, having died to sins, might live for righteousness—by whose stripes you were healed.

Romans 8:11

But if the Spirit of Him who raised Jesus from the dead dwells in you, He who raised Christ from the dead will also give life to your mortal bodies through His Spirit who dwells in you.

Romans 8:32

He who did not spare His own Son, but delivered Him up for us all, how shall He not with Him also freely give us all things?

Psalms 91:3 (NLT)

For He will rescue you from every trap and protect you from deadly disease.

Matthew 8:2–3 (NLT)

Suddenly, a man with leprosy approached Him and knelt before Him. "Lord," the man said, "if You are willing, You can heal me and make me clean." Jesus reached out and touched him. "I am willing," He said. "Be healed!" And instantly the leprosy disappeared.

Psalm 107:19–20 (NLT)

"Lord, help!" they cried in their trouble, and He saved them from their distress. He sent out His word and healed them, snatching them from the door of death.

Psalm 105:37

He also brought them out with silver and gold, and there was none feeble among His tribes.

3 John 1:2 (NASB)

Beloved, I pray that in all respects you may prosper and be in good health, just as your soul prospers.

John 10:10

"The thief does not come except to steal, and to kill, and to destroy. I have come that they may have life, and that they may have [it] more abundantly."

Psalm 103:2–3

Bless the Lord, O my soul, and forget not all His benefits: Who forgives all your iniquities, Who heals all your diseases.

Proverbs 4:20-22

My son, give attention to my words; incline your ear to my sayings. Do not let them depart from your eyes; keep them in the midst of your heart; for they [are] life to those who find them, and health to all their flesh.

Psalm 91:5-7 (NLT) Do not be afraid of the terrors of the night, nor the arrow that flies in the day. Do not dread the disease that stalks in darkness, nor the disaster that strikes at midday. Though a thousand fall at your side, though ten thousand are dying around you, these evils will not touch you.

Psalm 91:16

With long life I will satisfy him, and show him My salvation.

Exodus 15:26

"…I am the Lord who heals you."

Jeremiah 30:17 (NLT)

"I will give you back your health and heal your wounds," says the Lord.

Matthew 4:23

Everyone Who Came To Jesus Was Healed

And Jesus went about all Galilee, teaching in their synagogues, preaching the gospel of the kingdom, and healing all kinds of sickness and all kinds of disease among the people.

Matthew 4:24 (NLT)

News about Him spread as far as Syria, and people soon began bringing to Him all who were sick. And whatever their sickness or disease, or if they were demon-possessed or epileptic or paralyzed—He healed them all.

Matthew 9:6–7 (NLT)

...Then Jesus turned to the paralyzed man and said, "Stand up, pick up your mat, and go home!" And the man jumped up and went home!

Matthew 8: 5–7 (NIV)

When Jesus had entered Capernaum, a centurion came to him, asking for help. "Lord," he said, "my servant lies at home paralyzed and in terrible suffering." Jesus said to him, "I will go and heal him."

Matthew 8:16–17

When evening had come, they brought to Him many who were possesed with devils: And He cast out the spirits with his word, and healed all that were sick: that it might be fulfilled which was spoken by Esaias the prophet, saying, Himself took our infirmities, and bare our sicknesses.

Matthew 15:30

Then great multitudes came to Him, having with them [the] lame, blind, mute, maimed, and many others; and they laid them down at Jesus' feet, and He healed them.

Matthew 20:34 (NIV)

Jesus had compassion on them and touched their eyes. Immediately they received their sight and followed Him.

Mark 3:1–5

And He entered again into the synagogue; and there was a man there which had a withered hand. And they watched Him, whether He would heal him on the Sabbath day; that they might accuse Him.

And He saith unto the man which had the withered hand, "Stand forth". And he saith unto them, "Is it lawful to do good on the Sabbath days, or to do evil? to save life or to kill?" But they held their peace. And when He had looked around about on them with anger, being grieved by the hardness of their hearts, he saith unto the man, "Stretch forth thine hand." And he stretched it out: and his hand was restored whole as the other.

Mark 5:25–29 (NLT)

A woman in the crowd had suffered for twelve years with constant bleeding. She had suffered a great deal from many doctors, and over the years she had spent everything she had to pay them, but she had gotten no better. In fact, she had gotten worse. She had heard about Jesus, so she came up behind Him through the crowd and touched His robe. For she thought to herself, "If I can just touch His robe, I will be healed." Immediately the bleeding stopped, and she could feel in her body that she had been healed of her terrible condition.

Mark 10:49–52 (NIV)

Jesus stopped and said, "Call him." So they called to the blind man, "Cheer up! On your feet! He's calling you." Throwing his cloak aside, he jumped to his feet and came to Jesus. "What do you want Me to do for you?" Jesus asked him. The blind man said, "Rabbi, I want to see." "Go," said Jesus, "your faith has healed you." Immediately he received his sight and followed Jesus along the road.

Luke 4:40 (NJKV)

When the sun was setting, all those who had any that were sick with various diseases brought them to Him; and He laid His hands on every one of them and healed them.

Luke 6:19 (NKJV)

And the whole multitude sought to touch Him, for power went out from Him and healed [them] all.

Acts 10:38 (NKJV)

"…how God anointed Jesus of Nazareth with the Holy Spirit and with power, who went about doing good and healing all who were oppressed by the devil, for God was with Him."

Luke 7:12–15 (NLT)

A funeral procession was coming out as He approached the village gate. The young man who had died was a widow's only son, and a large crowd from the village was with her. When the Lord saw her, His heart overflowed with compassion. "Don't cry!" He said. Then He walked over to the coffin and touched it, and the bearers stopped. "Young man," He said, "I tell you, get up." Then the dead boy sat up and began to talk! And Jesus gave him back to his mother.

Luke 13:11–13 (NIV)

And a woman was there who had been crippled by a spirit for eighteen years. She was bent over and could not straighten up at all. When Jesus saw her, He called her forward and said to her, "Woman, you are set free from your infirmity." Then He put His hands on her, and immediately she straightened up and praised God.

John 5:5–9 (NLT)

One of the men lying there had been sick for thirty-eight years. When Jesus saw him and knew he had been ill for a long time, He asked him, "Would you like to get well?" "I can't, sir," the sick man said, "for I have no one to put me into the pool when the water bubbles up. Someone else always gets there ahead of me." Jesus told him, "Stand up, pick up your mat, and walk!" Instantly, the man was healed! He rolled up his sleeping mat and began walking!

Prayer For Healing And Wholeness

"Lord Jesus, I Thank You that You love me and that You are both able and willing to heal me. At the cross, You took all my sicknesses and pains in Your own body, and by Your stripes, I am healed! Your body was scourged and broken so that mine can be made whole. I receive all that You have done for me and I rest in Your finished work. There is nothing more for me to do. As I wait on You for the complete manifestation of my healing, I choose to focus on and give praise for Your great love for me. Amen.

About The Littles: A Restoration Story

Our story of Restoration is full of lessons learned on trust, forgiveness, true love and a willingness to change. If you knew us before, you would know that this is a huge transition from our first marriage which was filled with years of drug abuse, deceit, unfaithfulness and always wondering, 'Will this cycle ever end?'

Having taken this life's journey together we were married, divorced, and remarried! We have over 30 years of experience of marriage, family and ministry as well as overcoming addictions and having victory over things that can hold you captive.

We are the Founders of Lifestyle Soulutions, an Online Counseling Service that gives you clear soulutions for your life that will fix, recondition, and restore your lives and relationships because we care.

We have six beautiful children, eight wonderful grandchildren and one great-grandson.

We are both Ordained Ministers, Counselors and Inspiring Speakers who currently reside in Indiana.

To get the inside scoop-contact us! We would love to share our story!

Visit our website:

www.lifestylesoulutions.com

Email address:

lifestylesoulutions1@gmail.com

Social Media Information:

Facebook: Lifestyle Soulutions

Twitter: Lsoulutions

Instagram: lifestylesoulutions

Pinterest: Lifestyle Soulutions

YouTube: Lifestyle Soulutions

Made in the USA
Columbia, SC
03 October 2020

21970336R00067